MW00776694

Jobs For Felons

How to find employment if you have a criminal record.

Michael Ford

www.Felon-Jobs.Org

NEITHER THE PUBLISHER NOR AUTHOR MAKE ANY REPRESENTATIONS OR WARRANTIES WITH RESPECT TO THE ACCURACY OR COMPLETENESS OF THE CONTENTS OF THIS WORK AND SPECIFICALLY DISCLAIM ALL WARRANTIES, INCLUDING WITHOUT LIMITATION WARRANTIES OF FITNESS FOR A PARTICULAR PURPOSE. NO WARRANTY MAY BE CREATED OR EXTENDED BY SALES OR PROMOTIONAL MATERIALS. THE ADVICE AND STRATEGIES IN THIS WORK MAY NOT BE APPROPRIATE OR SUITABLE FOR EVERY SITUATION. THIS WORK IS SOLD WITH THE UNDERSTANDING THAT NEITHER THE PUBLISHER NOR THE AUTHOR ARE ENGAGED IN RENDERING LEGAL, ACCOUNTING, OR OTHER PROFESSIONAL SERVICES. IF PROFESSIONAL ASSISTANCE IS REQUIRED, THE SERVICES OF A COMPETENT PROFESSIONAL PERSON SHOULD BE SOUGHT. NEITHER THE PUBLISHER NOR THE AUTHOR SHALL BE LIABLE FOR DAMAGES ARISING FROM THE USE OF INFORMATION OR ADVICE IN THIS WORK. THE LISTING OF A WEBSITE, GROUP, OR ORGANIZATION IN THIS WORK DOES NOT CONSTITUTE ENDORSEMENT BY THE PUBLISHER OR AUTHOR. INTERNET WEBSITES LISTED IN THIS WORK MAY HAVE CHANGED OR DISAPPEARED SINCE THIS WORK WAS PUBLISHED.

EVERY REASONABLE ATTEMPT HAS BEEN MADE TO VERIFY THE ACCURACY OF THE INFORMATION IN THIS PROGRAM, HOWEVER NEITHER THE AUTHOR, PUBLISHER, NOR ANYONE ASSOCIATED WITH THE PRODUCTION OF THIS WORK ASSUMES ANY RESPONSIBILITY FOR ERRORS, INACCURACIES, OR OMISSIONS. THIS PROGRAM MAY MAKE SUGGESTIONS REGARDING MARKETING, SALES, AND ADVERTISING, WHICH ARE GOVERNED BY STATE LAWS WHICH MAY VARY. CHECK YOUR LOCAL LAWS AND THE RULES AND REGULATIONS OF EBAY. THE EBAY RULES AND REGULATIONS MAY HAVE CHANGED SINCE THIS PROGRAM WAS CREATED. SOME EBAY FEATURES REFERENCED IN THIS PROGRAM MAY HAVE CHANGED OR BEEN REMOVED SINCE THIS PROGRAM WAS PRODUCED.

eBay® is a trademark of eBay Inc. All other trademarks are property of their respective owners whether noted or not.

Jobs For Felons First Edition
Published by Elite Minds Inc, 355 N Lantana St #562, Camarillo CA 93010

ISBN 0-9774760-5-7
ISBN-13 978-0-9774760-5-3

Manufactured in the USA

©2009 Elite Minds Inc., All Rights Reserved.

No part of this publication may be reproduced, stored in a retrieval system or transmitted in any form or by any means, electronic, mechanical, photocopying, recording, scanning or otherwise, except as permitted under Sections 107 or 108 of the 1976 United States Copyright Act, without the prior written permission of the publisher.

For more information, bulk quantities, and other books, visit www.EliteMindsInc.com or www.Felon-Jobs.org

Introduction

Finding employment after being released from prison can be one of the most difficult tasks a felon faces. No one wants to hire you but parole terms require you to have a job or go back to jail. Even if you do not have parole requirements, you have to support yourself and face the question on every job applicatrion:

"HAVE YOU EVER BEEN CONVICTED OF A FELONY?"

Over 80% of all employers use some form of background check today which greatly limits the job paths available to convicted felons and even those convicted of misdemeanors.

Just because someone has a felony conviction does not necessarily make him or her a bad person. Unfortunately, most employers do not understand this distinction. There are many reasons, many valid reasons, someone can be convicted of a crime which can even result from them standing up for their rights or being in the wrong place at the wrong time. Many felony convictions are for non-violent offenses like failure to pay taxes, or refusing to testify against a friend, and similar offenses that are hardly crimes against humanity. Yet these poor souls are treated no differently from mass murders when it comes to finding jobs.

This guide will help ex-cons and their families by providing important information you can use to find employment and other resources to help you after release from jail or prison.

Attitude

The attitude you have when looking for a job is critical. You may quickly lose faith when you apply for three jobs and all three ask the dreaded question: "Have you ever been convicted of a crime?". You immediately know what the result will be when you answer and you feel like walking out without finishing the application. The result may not be what you think. Many companies will hire convicted felons depending on the crime and the amount of time that has passed. It is still true that having a conviction limits job opportunities but there are also other paths that many people never think about plus there are many organizations that specialize in helping ex-cons.

Even when things seem to be at their worst, try to keep a positive attitude. This attitude will show through when you go to interviews and you only have to impress one interviewer to get that job.

Never let yourself form the attitude of "They aren't going to hire me anyway so why bother." When you plant that poison in your mind you have set yourself up for failure. Every failure after this is the result of that attitude which only gives justification to strengthen the attitude. The person with this attitude never realizes the attitude itself comes through in their interviews and this negative attitude is why they are not being hired.

When you have a conviction, you have a harder struggle. Finding a job is difficult anyway so you must expect it to be more difficult with a conviction. If the average person goes to 10 interviews, then the felon may have to go to 100 interviews. It does not matter how many it takes, what is important is that you keep at it and you work to improve at each interview. Eventually it will pay off.

One of the worst mistakes you can make is to walk into a business and ask 'are you hiring' or 'do you have any jobs, I'll do anything'. Companies do not want people who will do anything. They want people who are interested in the company

4

and willing to do a good job. They want people who are motivated and interested in something specific.

Now, I know no one dreams of working as a janitor or in food preparation at a restaurant where they chop carrots all night and no one studies to become a waitress. But, those jobs require skills and the person who is a team player and wants to work at that specific business is more likely to be hired. If you are trying for a job as a waitress or waiter then say you enjoy being with people and love good food and a lively atmosphere. If you know a job in food prep is open then tell the owner that you are interested in being a chef someday and trying to break into food so you can learn. Telling a potential employer that you just want to pay your rent is not motivating for them and it sounds like you are just there to pick up a paycheck. No intelligent business owner will hire you if he thinks you are only there for him to give you money. He wants people who will work together with his team and people who want to do a good job they can be proud of at the end of the day.

Top Jobs For Felons

Delivery Driver

Many companies are willing to hire felons as delivery people as long as you have a clean driving record and no DUI's. UPS has been known to hire felons.

Join the Army

You may be able to join the Army or another military branch. It depends on the conviction you have. They will overlook some convictions and may be an option if you are under age 42.
You can find a link to the US Army policy on hiring felons at http://www.felon-jobs.org/resources/

Start your own business

This is one of the best options for ex-cons because you never have to go through a background check and never have to worry about being fired. The best businesses are low cost start-ups. Look for something you can do at home, on your computer, or something where people want to pay you to come to them. This avoids renting a storefront or office.
Some examples

- Windshield repair - People pay you to come to their house and repair dings in their windshield. You can purchase a kit, practice on windshields in a junkyard until you are good enough, then offer your services through your local free newspaper.
- Locksmith – There are many places where you can train to be a locksmith, even home study courses.
- You could become a barber and obtain a barber license. Opening a shop is expensive but what if you offered a 'we come to you' barber service. How many people would pay extra to have you come to their house and cut their hair or their children's hair?

The big advantage of starting your own business is that there are no background checks. I recommend you buy some books on starting your business and a book on creating a business plan. Some books on marketing your business and the difference between a sole-proprietorship and a corporation would also be a good idea. This is a huge topic and much too complicated to go into here but you must do some research and understand at least something about running a business before jumping in. The important thing to do is research and study business books first. Most businesses fail because the person who starts it knows nothing about business. They hope to hang out their sign and the money will come in. It never happens that way. You will need a plan and you should start small.

Telephone Customer Service

Many companies are willing to hire felons to handle phone based customer service. They will take the chance because you aren't dealing with the people in person which reduces the liability risk to the company. Also, many phone support jobs are difficult to fill and high turnover jobs. Technical support jobs are also difficult to fill because if someone actually knows anything about computers, they will not work phone support. If you know about computers or are willing to learn about a company's product, then they may be willing to let you work in phone support. You should avoid cold-call telemarketing companies. These are barely legal anyway and working every day at a job you know to be unethical while dealing with people who are angry you called them in the middle of dinner will only make you dislike the job.

Temp Agency

Temp agencies are a good option. You will have to explain what your conviction was for and convince them it will not affect your work. Some temporary employment agencies will not work with released felons but others will. Many companies, ones that would never consider hiring a felon full time, will hire people from a Temp Agency or even short term contract people without a background check.

Family Business

You may be able to work in a family or friend's business. They will be happy to hire you if you are willing to work hard and they will probably be glad to help you get back on your feet. This is a very good option if you must find a job quickly as part of your parole or probation requirements. You can always offer to work extra unpaid hours just to get a job. Once you have the job you can relax and look for a better job elsewhere if you do not want to continue in this one.

You may turn to friends and relatives who own businesses and offer to work for less money than they would pay someone else. This will make them want to hire you. Greed is strong and if they can pay you $3 an hour less, then it benefits them because they save money but more importantly it benefits you because you get the job you need. This is a job that you can use to find the next job. You never have to go to the next interview and say you are unemployed, instead you say you are interested in moving up

You may turn to friends and relatives who own businesses and offer to work for less money than they would pay someone else. This will make them want to hire you. Greed is strong and if they can pay you $3 an hour less, then it benefits them because they save money but more importantly it benefits you because you get the job you need. This is a job that you can use to find the next job. You never have to go to the next interview and say you are unemployed, instead you say you are interested in moving up

Independent Contractor

Most people will gladly use your services as long as you get the job done. If you work hard, it doesn't matter that you have a felony on your record and they will never ask. Most states require a license of some sort for handy-man type work. If you are unable to obtain a license, then you may find work with someone who does have a license and needs a helper. You can also look at doing specialty work, such as septic tank work, or cutting house rafters. Many construction companies may have no interest in hiring you for 'just anything' but if you let them know you are experienced in septic tank problems, they may call you in on those specialty jobs.

Truck Driver

It is a myth that trucking companies are willing to hire all felons or that there is always a demand for felons in the trucking industry. These jobs ares also difficult to obtain because special licensing is required for larger trucks. If you are on parole this kind of work may not be possible because the job will likely require you to go out of state. If you are not on parole then this would not be a problem. Truck driving jobs are not a sure thing and if you lack experience it is unlikely you will be able to drive an 18 wheeler, maybe smaller trucks.

There are many delivery jobs that do not involve the big 18 wheelers which you can apply for. You can also attend a truck driving school which will help you obtain work. Smaller truck driving companies hire ex-cons because they need workers. If you contact a school, ask them about job placement for felons. You can also call truck driving companies and ask if they hire felons to see if there is any chance you would be hired if you did go through truck driving school.

Since 9/11, the Federal government has placed a seven year time restriction on persons with felony convictions before they can get their HazMat endorsements. Some states, NY, in particular, require ten years from the time of conviction. However, I would not discount companies that have straight frame (or B-class) trucks either.

Medical Tests

It may not sound glamorous, maybe even scary, but it pays real money and they do not ask any questions other than health related ones. There are many medical studies going on around the country. These are not all for cancer or heard disease either. Somewhere a company has a new product that heals scars. They want people with scars who will try their product and let them photograph the results.

Some company has a new tattoo removal system and they need people to test it on. Some of these jobs are outpatient type jobs where they pay you a few hundred dollars a month. Others are in-patient where you are kept in a hospital and monitored. These pay the most and may involve testing new drugs, anti depressants, or they may simply want to see how a healthy person reacts to an anti-inflammatory drug. You may even be one of the people who receive the placebo drug that does nothing and not the real drug. Check the Internet or if you have a local teaching hospital or research center they may be able to help too.

Privately Owned Small Businesses

Larger companies and chain stores have rules against hiring felons. Small business owners are more likely to hire people they like regardless of their background. They will take more of a 'risk' in hiring employees, and you can strike a personal note with the business owner that you never could with a human resources person representing a chain store.

#1 Recommended Job - Online Freelance Work

This is the best job for a felon because it requires no background check, no drug tests, no psychological tests, no certifications or anything else. You are hired based on what you can do and nothing else matters. You never see an employer face to face and are hired over the Internet by a real company to do one job.

I am talking about remote, work at home type jobs. Not the fake jobs you see on the Internet like those assemble-junk-at-home jobs or copying names from the phone book type jobs, or stuffing envelope jobs, those are all scams. There are no such jobs in existence. There are however many legitimate work at home opportunities where small companies hire you online and pay up-front. These companies need a specific job completed. It may be a technical job like creating a website or a basic skills job like data entry or web research. These jobs may last a day, a week, or a month. You can work multiple jobs at once if you want or you can take a break or vacation anytime you feel like it. If you only want to work one day a week, you can do it. You have complete control over how much you make and when you work and you never have to go to a job interview again.

If you are good with computers that helps but it is not necessary. These jobs vary depending on what the company needs. You work for one company a few days then work for the next company. You pick the job you want and what you want to be paid in advance of accepting the job. The jobs range from computer programming, to data entry, webpage design, editing and proofreading, recording voicemail welcome messages, editing video, doing web research, forum marketing, writing sales letters, and anything else that can be done remotely.

These freelance jobs are posted on special Hire-Me Network sites by companies around the world. You look through the listings and pick a job you want, then tell the company what you want to be paid and when you can complete the job.

This is a simple system, however, many people make common mistakes which prevent them from being hired. It is just like the real world where many people make mistakes on a resume or cover letter or during an interview and are not hired. In the Internet world, you must know how to act and how to respond to these job postings otherwise you will not be hired.

Would you go to a job interview, stick your head in the door, toss a handwritten piece of paper with your phone number on it on the desk of the human resources person and say *"I can do it, Hire me"* then walk away? That would be absolutely stupid and the employer would have no reason to hire such a person. Yet, people who do not understand how etiquette on the Hire-Me freelance sites work do exactly this every day.

This opens the door for you and if you know some inside secrets about how these sites work, you can gain a great advantage over many other job seekers on these sites.

I highly recommend you go through a special video course which explains exactly how these freelance sites work and how you can gain instant employment through them anytime you want. If you have even basic computer skills then I absolutely recommend that you complete the online video training course which will prepare you for these remote, work-at-home jobs.

You can find out more about the Hire-Me Network Video Course at http://www.felon-jobs.com/jobs-for-felons/

Work Outside The USA

Have you considered working in another country? Can you speak(or are you willing to learn) another language? Do some research and find what jobs are hot in a country you want to work in. Employers in some countries are more likely to hire an American with a felony conviction than other countries. Some countries also have privacy laws which may restrict what questions the employer can ask.

You will have to obtain a work permit or work visa to go with your passport so this is not as simple as applying for a job in your home country. Some countries will not issue a visa(the permission required to enter the country) to those convicted of felonies so you will need to check on this and see if the requirement expires after so many years too.

Some countries require visa approval or a Certificate Of Good Conduct. You can find information on how to obtain these at

http://www.felon-jobs.org/resources/

> *Note: The Peace Corps is a government organization and not a non-profit. They are very strict and will reject people with misdemeanor convictions and even those with no convictions if they have an arrest history.*

Landscaping

Landscaping companies often need workers who are willing to put in a long day and do physical labor. They may want you to mow lawns or other low skill jobs. If you have experience driving heavy equipment, laying brick, or similar skills these can help too.

Manual Labor

Commercial fishing, road construction, any strenuous job that is hard to fill and has a high turnover rate is a possibility.

> Note: If your probation forbids you from associating with other convicted felons, look for jobs that are not commonly sought after by ex-cons. You may also want to ask your employer if other felons are working with you and explain that you are not supposed to associate with them.

Counselor

You can work as a counselor in many states. A counselor usually does not require any state certification but this also depends on the type of counseling. You can often take an Internet or correspondence course for a diploma or certificate. Having a criminal conviction often is beneficial for a substance abuse counselor because you can relate directly to those you are trying to help in some way. You may be competing with people who have college degrees, however your first hand experience can give you an advantage plus your willingness to work part time, nights, or for lower pay than a college graduate may expect can help too. Working as a volunteer counselor(no pay) can also give you something to do where you help others and letting prospective employers know this is how you spend your time can also help during a job interview. You may also work to assist a counselor or in a support role. Check the non profit organizations in your city.

Sales Jobs

It is hard for companies to find good sales people. If you have ever gone to a mall and asked the teenage girl behind the counter for help then you know what I mean. A good car salesman is worth his weight in gold. There are many home based courses and books that teach salesmanship. You can purchase one of these courses, practice your skills at your own yard sale, then go to a local car dealer and show off your skills to the manager. If he is impressed, he may not care about a conviction in the past.

Chef

If you are passionate about cooking then you may be able to find work as a chef. Restaurants rarely do background checks and if you can show some passion and skill they may give you a chance. Offer to work one night for free as an assistant so they can see how you do with no obligations. You may work for 10 free nights before you find a job but now you have a job. You do not have to attend a culinary school, just research what being a chef requires. Do not expect to be hired as a head chef either. You will be an assistant, but once you learn how it works you may find you are going to other restaurants to see if they have a head chef position open while explaining your current experience.

A word of warning, many culinary schools are not honest. They will make you any promise they need to get you to sign for a loan including, even lying about how much it will cost a month to repay. Before attending any culinary school, talk to past graduates who had to pay back loans and see if the education is worthwhile, if they are helpful in finding employment, or if you are better off buying some home study courses and videos.

Federal Jobs

Being an ex-offender does not prevent you from obtaining Federal Employment. Your past record will be considered as part of the decision process in determining your suitability but there are no general prohibitions against hiring you. Government agencies consider a number of factors such as the duties of the positions requested, the nature of the crime, how long ago it occurred, and any evidence of rehabilitation.

There are some regulations which will prohibit you from working in certain positions if you have a specific conviction. The most common situation involves being convicted of misdemeanor domestic violence crimes under Federal or State law. These persons are prohibited from working in any position that requires the individual to ship, transport, possess, or receive firearms or ammunition (Public Law 1-4-208 Omnibus Consolidated Appropriations Act of 1997)

Other laws or regulatory restrictions exist, but rarely apply. You can be excluded from Federal employment for such offenses as treason, inciting rebellion against the U.S., willful and unlawful destruction of public records, or knowingly and willfully advocating the overthrow of the U.S. Government. It is important that you provide all the required information about your criminal record when you apply for Federal employment. Then the employing agency can determine quickly if a specific prohibition exists which prevents you from wasting your time

14

or getting your hopes up.

Some federal jobs are out of reach because of the education and background requirements. There is a seven year waiting list for Park Rangers in some areas. Some federal jobs have long waiting lists and special training requirements even if they may seem like they are easy to those who have not done the work. Being a park ranger seems like easy work, walk in the woods, but it actually requires a great deal of education before you are even considered.

Freelance Journalist/Photographer

If you have journalism experience or if you are just willing to learn, then you can become a freelance journalist or photographer. You are not employed full time by any news service but you instead find out what they want stories on then interview people and write stories for their magazine, newspaper, or website. Websites can be the best because they need the most content though they may pay less per article. Many photographers grab photos of events or celebrities and sell those to newspapers. You can take home-study courses or attend your local community college on journalism. You will need good writing and grammar skills.

Independent Worker Jobs

Some companies look for distributors or people willing to work independently. For example, a carpet cleaning company may send you on jobs as an independent contractor(but you have to buy the equipment and give them a cut of the fee). Retail service companies may use you as an independent contractor to go around to their locations and check equipment, do basic service like adding cups or checking for damage.

Flea Markets

There are no background checks on people who setup in flea markets. If you are into antiques, if you produce crafts or furniture that can be sold, anything that you can do at a flea market is open territory. You can buy at one flea market and sell at another. You can troll the garage sales one weekend and sell your found treasures at the flea market or even on eBay. It is difficult to work full time at this but it is a possibility that many pursue.

Ebay

Anyone can start buying and selling on eBay. There is an advantage with online auction sites, a ready supply of buyers. If you setup a store then you have to convince buyers to come in. On eBay the buyers are there looking for items to buy. An eBay business also has the advantage that you can work from home at least most of the time, there are no background checks, and it is even something you can do when you have a part time job to generate additional income. Running online auctions does require some knowledge. Visit www.dontbidonit.com for information on setting up your own eBay business and what is involved. The Don't Bid On It course contains a great deal of information not available elsewhere.

Manual Labor

Manual labor is one way to go. The pay is decent and years of experience isn't necessary. They may require less than a specified number of felonies and certain amount of time must have passed since the last one.

Food Services

Restaurants, fast food, donut shops, and especially smaller non-chain eateries in smaller towns. Wait tables if you can, and then you can get tips. Save your money and start looking for your next job. You can also offer to do part-time work. Sometimes these places need help on the weekend only. Some may need help on Mondays only. If you can work at two or three places at different times then you have a survivable income.

Apprenticeships

People can be paid to assist a professional and in the process they the trade and even get licensed in the process. There is more information on Apprenticeships in the Recently Released Prisoner Handbook. You can find information on obtaining a free copy at the end of this book.

Telemarketing and Mystery Shopping

There is no such thing as an honest cold-call telemarketing job and for every legitimate Mystery Shopper job, there are 1000 scams to steal your identity or trick you into paying a fee. Cold-call telemarketing is a sleazy business and after you are cursed out by 100 people in a day you will have little left when you go home. Take an honest job instead. Don't waste your time with these.

Avon

Ex-cons can become Avon representatives. The same is true for many similar distribution companies..

Research

Do some research before you are in too deep. If you are interested in any of these jobs or if you have your own idea, then talk to some people in the industry FIRST. You do not want to take an Internet course on some subject, spend a month or more studying, only to find out that there are no local jobs for your new skill or to find out that the companies near you do not hire felons no matter what. Make some calls and see if you could get work in your newly chosen field as a felon before investing your time and effort into a new career path.

It's All About Who You Know

You have heard the saying and I bet you believe it, "It's all about who you know." This is not completely true but it can help. The question then becomes how do you get to know those right people.

Two answers are *Volunteer Work* and *Join A Church*.

These are two places where you can meet other people who are willing to help you. You can volunteer and help out in a church of your choice to establish that you are a trustworthy person and you can meet many community leaders here. Churches are social centers where you can meet people in a way that is not possible elsewhere and you meet people who are usually willing to help you. If one church does not work, you can always join another.

As a volunteer you can show your willingness to work and help others plus the right kind of volunteer work will put you in touch with many businesses including small businesses where the owner makes hiring decisions himself based on who he likes.

You can also consider professional and social organizations like the Civitan Club, Kawanas and other similar organizations. You can meet many important people in places like these.

When you are networking at an event, church, or a club, you want to make your first priority to establish relationships. You should never walk around asking people if they have a job. This is a slow process. They need to get to know you well first. If you are on the clock and have to get a job to satisfy your release terms, this is not the way. If you are trying to re-establish yourself in society then this is a good way. You can slowly build relationships that will help you later.

No Lists

There is no list of ex-con friendly employers. Even big companies do not usually hire a lot of new people all of the time. Certainly they do not hire as many felons as are released each day. Big companies also do not want to be known as companies that hire felons. The company that hires three felons this week may not hire any new employees for months too. Any list of companies that hired felons would be outdated and inaccurate the instant it was completed because the jobs available would be filled, companies would change policies, etc. Don't waste
18

your time looking for a magical list of companies that hire felons, no such thing exists.

Non Profit Companies That Help

You can find help through non profit organizations that specialize in this area. In southern California you can try
http://www.changelives.org/home.html
In Chicago try
http://www.saferfoundation.org/viewpage.asp?id=4
You can check with Goodwill anywhere because they try to help the disadvantaged and disabled http://www.goodwill.org and United Way may be helpful http://www.unitedway.com

Another organization that helps drug addicts and ex-convicts and has offices in a number of states is
http://www.delanceystreetfoundation.org/
They actually do not offer jobs but can provide unpaid training.
Check your local Job Service office too. They frequently have special jobs available to felons. Many employers simply need a strong back and on their job forms they say they will hire ex-cons. This makes it easy for you because you know in advance they do not care about your background.
You can find resources at the Legal Action Center
 http://www.lac.org/
which will help you rebuild your life.
Another possible resource in California is
http://www.Theworkplaceca.com
Career One Stop can help with placement of ex-cons too
http://www.careeronestop.com/

**You can find an updated list at
http://www.felon-jobs.org/resources/**

19

Education

Try to go to college. When you come out of prison, you may have no money which makes you a potential candidate for student loans or even grants(you do not have to pay back grants). This is a good opportunity to improve your education which makes it easier to find a job plus being in college it is natural for companies to hold job fairs on campus where you can apply. Colleges often have job placement assistance or co-op programs that allow students to work one semester with companies that hire students as part of the program and go to school the next. For more information on paying for college and for many ways to go to college for free, visit
http://free-college.y3s.net

College is also a good option because when you are ready to apply for a new job, you never have to answer the question "Why did you leave your last job." Even if you only take a vocational course for 2 or 3 semesters, you have an honest answer to what you have been doing for the past year.

If you cannot afford to go to college but want to improve your education, you can visit your local library. They often have audio and video programs of college level courses. Just sit and watch or listen in the library. You can also find many audio and video courses on the Internet, some free and some you can purchase. These can give you skills or at least teach you enough so you can get a new, better job. If you can walk into a sign shop and tell them what you know about silk screening then they may be interested in hiring you to do silk screening. Even if you have no experience, you can watch online videos and learn how the process works. If you plan to go to college later, you can also use the college audio and video courses which teach math, history, science to gain an advantage by learning the material before the actual course.

Working for large companies may still present a problem because of the background check, but there are many smaller and start-up companies that do not use background checks. You may also find students who are starting their own companies and will hire you based on knowing you so you are in on the ground floor of the business.

Mental Conditions

Are you bi-polar?

Are you sure? Doctors often mis-diagnose many problems. The symptoms of bi-polar disorder can also be present with many other diseases and conditions. If you have been diagnosed with ANY mental disorder, do your own research and seek a second opinion. It could be something else. I once saw a woman who was clearly schizophrenic. She was incoherent and talked to people and things that were not there, she was paranoid. Anyone could see she was schizophrenic and that is exactly what her doctor diagnosed. However, it turned out years later that she was not schizophrenic! She had a thyroid gland problem and the symptoms looked the same. With a simple medication her problem was solved and she was normal the next day.

You are facing a handicap if you have a mental disorder when it comes to finding work but you have an even bigger handicap if you have a different disorder than you thought or if you have no problems at all and think you do, or if you had a problem in the past and are still medicating yourself but the problem has changed or become less severe.

If you do have a mental disorder which makes finding employment difficult, I would again recommend freelance type work through the Hire-Me Network of sites because you never have to deal with employers face to face and they pay based on the job you do only. You can work when you are able, take a break when you want. You never have to deal with customers or co-workers face to face either. If you lack computer skills, then you may find it is worthwhile to learn those skills just to do this type of freelance work.

If you have mental handicaps, are bipolar or have a similar problem, you can look into job placement services like your local Job Services office. These often have connections to state programs that give federal aid to people classified as mentally handicapped (including bipolar) so they can go back to school. They pay tuition and, often, living expenses. You can find some information about how to go to college and many ways to go to college for free at http://free-college.y3s.net

Interview Secrets

Sending out stacks of resumes hoping someone will respond is a mistake and a waste of time. Most of them will go in the garbage, the rest will go in a shredder.

Unless you are applying for a specific job and you have specific skills, no one will look twice at a resume that comes in the mail especially if they receive a stack of them every day. They will not even look at long enough to see if there is a mention of a felony conviction. You may have some hope if you send a good cover letter to a business that does not receive stacks of applications every day.

The personal touch always helps. Employers hire people they like, not descriptions on a resume. You can call or stop by but don't act like you are just there to get something from them or act like you are entitled to or expect a job just for showing up.

Pick up a copy of the book <u>Dress For Success.</u> It will help you when it comes to dressing for a job interview. You want to look good, but not better than the person interviewing you.

Honesty

I am not a lawyer and I am not giving any legal advice. However, based on my understanding I want to share what I believe to be general knowledge that will help you.

You are handed an application to fill out and as you sit down and lick the tip of your pencil you see the first question in big letters

"Have you ever been convicted of a felony Y/N?"

I know the thought went through your mind saying,

"Hey, if I say yes I don't get the job and if I say No I may get the job. If I say No and they do a background check then it would not matter because I would not have gotten the job anyway."

When you are asked if you are a felon on a job application, you can lie and say NO. It may or may not be illegal depending on the state and is usually a civil matter anyway. You see, lying itself is not a crime, only when it is perjury or fraud does it become a crime. There are some problems with this though. What if you are hired and then your life goes well, your job goes well, you move up in the company and become a respected employee. Then, ten years after you are hired, you are recommended to become president of the company. Now the guy you beat out for the job is mad so he does some checking and finds out that you have a conviction but lied on your original application. He brings this up at the next board meeting and you are immediately fired, all of your hard work is down the drain and you have a new black spot on your record. No matter how good you were at your job, no matter how honest the last 10 years were, no company will want anything to do with you.

You should not leave the question blank. That will make the interviewer think you have something to hide. You should not try to fill in a lengthy explanation. That will look like you are trying to explain it away and distract the interviewer from a simple Yes. You can write Yes or "Yes, please ask during interview for details." when faced with this dreaded question.

If you are applying for a federal or government job and lie on the application, that is a crime. If you apply for some jobs like daycare, at a school, a job that requires special certification(like a paramedic or nurse), a job that requires you to carry or deal with firearms, or similar jobs, then it may be a crime so serious you could go back to jail just for putting NO on the application.

What happens if you lie, get the job, then a parole officer shows up asking questions at the employer's office? You will look dishonest and the employer will feel like he was played and will likely fire you on the spot for lying on the job application. Even if you are not on parole, what happens if a crime is committed similar to the one you were convicted of? Then the police will see who was recently released from prison and show up to ask some questions. Now everyone knows anyway and again you will likely be fired for lying on your application.

Lying on an application to get a job or faking credentials to get a higher paying job can be considered fraud because you lied in order to get money for the job or to get more money by claiming you had training or certification you did not have.

> *Jane: "I am afraid I lied on my application and I got the job. Now the company wants to do a background check on all employees. I have only been here six months. What should I do?"*

> *Jane has three options 1. let them run the background check and wait to be fired, 2. come clean and hope her employer is understanding, or 3. quit. The best option may be to simply resign and tell your co-workers you want to do something different with your life. This avoids a firing and you can honestly tell your next potential employer that you resigned your last job and left of your own free will to pursue a new career path.*

If you are asked by an employer "Do you have any convictions in the past 7 years" then the honest answer may be No. However the real answer is "No, but...", especially if you just were released and are on parole. In this case, you must explain that you were just released because your probation officer will verify employment anyway. This is not a "don't ask, don't tell" situation. If you honestly say no and your parole officer calls to verify, now you look like a liar and may be fired even though you told the truth. If you are not on probation and no one will check, then tell the truth, say No. Some states do require you to notify an employer if you are on active probation or parole. Many companies do not conduct background checks beyond 7 years.

Note: As of my last check, Wal-Mart does not hire anyone with a felony conviction unless it is at least 7 years in the past but may make exceptions for some types of felonies. The local stores may not even know about their own policies and managers may make up policies on the spot. Try applying online instead and check the option to work as a temp or part time. When you are asked to fill out a form listing convictions, just be honest and list them all. If they called you then they are interested in hiring you. Many times the form may never be processed, may be lost, or no one may look at it before the hiring decision is made.

Staples has hired felons. Apply online and then visit the store a day or two later to let them know you applied online. This and other companies(depending on the state) will hire ex-cons in order to receive a tax credit.

Honesty is the best policy. If they ask, tell them, but make sure to tell your side of the story and let them know you are leaving the past in the past and show them concrete examples of how your life has changed. They need more than just a promise to do better, tell the potential employer things you have actually done toward the creation of your new life, action you have taken, not just plans you have made.

TIP: If your felony conviction is over 7 years old, most states don't allow background checks to go beyond that date. If your state has this law, you can answer 'no' on an application because the question only applies to the past 7 years even if it does not specifically say 7 years. This does not apply to some jobs such as jobs that require you to carry a firearm or work with children so check your state law carefully.

25

TIP: If you have lived in a state more than 7 years and it has been 7 years or more since your conviction and have never been convicted of a crime in your current state(your felony conviction was at the state level, not federal, and the crime was in another state), then you may be able to answer NO because the question often applies only to the current state. If your resume and work history make no reference to the state where your conviction occurred, the company may not check your background in that state.

Tattoos

If you have any visible tattoos, get rid of them. They will prevent you from getting hired at any white collar company. Even if it is expensive, even if it is painful, even if it takes time, get rid of all visible tattoos and it will help your job search a lot. Covering them up with a bandage is not a good idea. First, you have to lie if the interviewer asks what the bandage is for. Second, if you are hired then the company will see your tattoos and feel that you tried to deceive them and wonder what else you did not tell them. Just get rid of the problem and you will find it easier to sit in front of an interviewer. If you absolutely cannot afford to have a visible tattoo on your neck or face removed, try to have it covered by a new tattoo to look like a birthmark or see if a tattoo artist can put a lighter color over it to make it less noticable.

Background Checks

There are three kinds of background checks. Checks in a current state. Checks in all states. Federal checks. Many employers only do background checks for the current state or for all states looking for state level convictions. Many commercial databases do not contain federal conviction records but only federal prison sentences. This means that if you only served federal probation and never served time in a federal prison, your record may not even show up. You should find out by purchasing a background check on yourself to see what comes back. If there is an error, you will need to have it corrected. Errors are common.

You can check your own record through the same commercial services used by many employers with the link below plus it has information on obtaining a copy of your FBI file if you were investigated by the FBI or if you have a federal conviciton and it has information on checking your record for international travel and those restrictions.

http://www.felon-jobs.com/resources/

The cost is very reasonable. You should also purchase your own record from more than one company. Different companies use different databases. You may not show up in one database at all while another may have your records. You need to know what a potential employer will see when he does a background check before you try applying for a job.

You should also obtain copies of your credit reports. You can obtain these free online, once per year from each of the 3 reporting agencies. There are many companies claiming to offer free credit reports but to get the *free* report you must pay them to signup for a monthly program of some kind. Do not fall for this trick. Your credit reports can be requested for FREE once a year. You can find more information at the FTC. You can also find links at http://www.felon-jobs.com/resources/

Ex-cons are the targets of identity theft very frequently. Your social security number has passed through the hands of many people plus if your friends or family had access to your information and any of them are untrustworthy they may have seen your incarceration as an opportunity to exploit. Most identity theft occurs with family and friends. Make sure you check your report.

When most employers run a background check on you, they also check your credit report. If you have no activity for the past 7 years(which is the limit on reporting), that looks fishy. If your bank offers a debit card that is linked to a major credit card company, get it. Once you have it then you can apply for a low limit credit card. You can also ask your bank about getting a real credit card(not a debit card). Many banks offer both cards and if you have an account in good standing, they may help you get a card through them. This will establish some activity on your record so you do not look like a ghost who just appeared out of nowhere one day. Hopefully your prison address is not on your report. If it is, it will eventually drop off or be pushed far down by new entries as you exercise credit wisely.

Banks, car insurance companies, and others will also check your credit record if you do not already have an established account with them.

Applications and Interviews

When filling out job applications and you are asked for your last income and you worked a prison job(which usually pays less than $1 an hour), do not list the amount. Just put in *Minimum Wage*. Whatever you were paid, it was the minimum legally allowable by the state so this is true.

Avoid using negative terms like "was convicted" or "jail" or "criminal". Try to make it sound more businesslike. Don't even mention jail or prison if you can avoid it. Most people do not know the difference between parole and probation so if you say your parole expired two years ago or your parole will expire in six months the interviewer may assume you never served time and were on probation. Do not say you were "convicted" say you were "sentenced as a result of a plea deal" which is very businesslike, or if you were found guilty just say "sentenced". Avoid volunteering anything, especially negative details, if you do not have to. You do not want to appear as if you are holding back so be conversational, volunteer some positive comments but do not go into detail or give unnecessary negative details.

When listing previous work experience, you may have a big gap in your work history during the time you served. You can draw attention away from this by not listing jobs in chronological order but instead list them in relevance to the current job sought. This will make it harder for the interviewer to see a gap. You can also split each job up and instead of listing companies, list your experience by area. This allows you to list the same company more than once. For example, if you worked at Acme Inc and started in the shipping department by identifying which boxes shipped where, then moved to office manager of the shipping department, that is two jobs which might look like this:

> **Office Manager – Managed incoming shipments and personnel used to process and ship boxes, Acme Inc, 2001**
> ...other experiences...
> **Shipping Clerk – Processed incoming and outgoing packages to verify they went to the correct locations when they arrived on the dock, Acme Inc, 2000**

During an interview, never be timid or apologetic when asked about your criminal history. Talk matter-of-factly about it. These are the facts and it is all in the past, do you have any other questions? If an interviewer sees you recoil, panic, or clam up when asked about your history he will not trust you. Instead, be open, lean forward, open your arms and tell him your side. This is a good opportunity to tell the interviewer what you learned and how it has made you a better person plus how you can use this experience to contribute to their company.

It is important to practice this interview before going to a real interview. This means practicing with someone if possible or at least with yourself in a mirror. If possible, record your interview on video and watch it afterward. This will help you see what your interview looks like. It may not be what you thought it looked like either. Now you can improve and you will be prepared for the real interview.

If you are asked by the interviewer, *"I see you listed Yes for the felony conviction, tell me about that.*" you may respond something like this:

> "I'm glad you asked because I want you to understand the situation so you can feel comfortable hiring me. It is embarrassing for me to talk about. I want to assure you that it had nothing to do with my previous employers. I took some things that didn't belong to me and as a result, it was a foolish thing but since then I've taken the time to decide what field I would like to get into and made some important decisions about the direction of my life. I have enrolled in several clerical courses and can type 50 wpm. I am familiar with several business software programs, and have excellent phone skills. I am very interested in learning all I can about this industry, and I know I would be an asset to your organization."

Notice how this ended in a very positive statement. The job seeker did not give a short one line answer which would have sounded negative. This job seeker covered the issue and continued until the interviewer may have even forgotten what question he had asked.

Here is another good response:

> "When I was younger I got mixed up with the wrong crowd and got in trouble when we were breaking into cars. We all do things when we are young that we regret. I used the time to my advantage by completing an air conditioning and heating training program and received my certificate. I've researched several air conditioning companies in the area and yours is well respected. I would really like to be a part of your team and I know I can do a job that will make your customers happy."

OR

> "In my past, I was involved with drugs, but since that period I've taken control of my life and put it behind

me. I have been clean for three years and have no desire to return to that life. I have two years of experience in food service and want to stay in this industry and ultimately I would like to become a chef. I am sure you know that, as a result of my past, when you hire me, your company is eligible for the Work Opportunity Tax Credit, which can save you up to $2,400. Are you familiar with this program?"

Advice For Answering The
"Felony Interview Question"

Sandwich your response. Explain your felony conviction in between several strengths and accomplishments. People often remember the first and last parts of sentences and ignore the rest.

Own up. Be honest.

Think about how you would answer these questions:
> What strengths and accomplishments do I have?
> How do I feel about what I did?
> How have I changed as a result of going to prison?
> Where am I going?
> What are my life and career plans?

When you receive the answer about the hiring decision, always:

> ➢ Be polite. Whether you get the results you want or not, thank the person for taking the time to speak with you.(You never know, they may have another opening soon and remember you.)

> ➢ Be prepared to answer questions about your background and/or experience.

➤ Have a pen and paper handy to take down information or directions.

➤ Be prepared to set up an interview.

EXAMPLES OF ILLEGAL INTERVIEW QUESTIONS(From the Federal Bureau of Prisons)

These are questions that should NOT be asked in an interview by an employer:

- Are you married?
- How old are you?
- Do you have children?
- What is your sexual preference?
- Do you go to church?
- Do you have a disability? If so, what is it?
- How much do you weigh?
- How tall are you?
- Is your childcare taken care of and who is your provider?
- Do you own your home or rent?
- Do you plan on having children/more children?
- Would you like to go out with me?
- Tell us something about any personal, family, or health issues that will prevent you from doing your job.
- What does your spouse do?
- What political party do you belong to?
- How much money did you make last year?
- Have you been arrested and if so, what was the charge?
- What is your opinion on (politics, social groups, religion)?
- Do you drink, take drugs, both?

If you are asked any illegal question, your options include the following:

- Answer the question
- Gently refuse to answer the question
- Change the subject
- Make a "joke" about the question (Be Careful - this can be difficult)
- Return the question to the interviewer with another question:
  o "That is interesting, why do you ask?"
- Look confused and ask "I'm sorry, does this apply to the job?"
  o "If I don't answer, will I automatically not get the job?"
- Not recommended: "Are you aware that you have just asked me an illegal question?"

Difficult Questions Employers Might Ask

During an interview, an employer is trying to get as much information about you as possible in a very short amount of time. Below is a list of difficult questions that an employer might ask you. Take some time and write out your answers on a sheet of paper to see how you would answer them.

1) I've noticed gaps in your work history; can you explain those gaps?
2) Have you ever been convicted of a crime?
3) What were your convictions?
4) What have you learned from this?
5) How can you assure our company that you won't re-offend or commit the same crime?

Examples of Other Difficult Interview Questions

1) Tell us about yourself.

2) Why do you want to work here?

3) Why did you leave your last job?

4) Name three strengths and three weaknesses.

5) How do you respond to having to work under pressure?

6) How many days of work did you miss in the last year?

7) I see on your application that you have had many jobs in the past year; is there a reason for this?

8) Would you have any objections if we contacted any of your former employers?

9) Where do you see yourself five years from now? What are your long-range career plans?

10) Why should I hire you?

11) What would you do if there were a conflict between you and a supervisor? What would you do if there were a conflict between you and another worker?

12) Why do you want to work for our company?

Many felons have a difficult time finding a job before their conviction. It becomes harder after a conviction. This is usually due to no job skills or no communication skills or a combination of the two. If this is you, then you may need to work on your people skills before you attend an interview. When you are applying for a job, you must sell yourself. You can never assume your resume will convince an employer to hire you. You can never assume that you will be hired just because a job is open either.

Follow-Up Calls To The Employer

After an interview, you will want to call the employer to follow-up.

Below are examples of phone scripts you can use when calling an employer to get more information about a job or to apply for a job.

For a Classified Ad:

> Hello, my name is _____(name)_____. I'm calling about the (Job title)_position advertised in (name of newspaper). I've had (number of years of experience or "a lot") years of experience in this field and would like to set up a time when we could discuss this job in more detail.

For a Random Call When No Position Has Been Advertised:

> Hello, my name is ____(name)_____. I'm calling to see if you have any openings for _(specific job you're interested in)_. I've had ___(number of years or "a lot")____ years of experience in this field and would like to set up a time when we could discuss this job in more detail.

If They Don't Have Openings:

> Would it be possible for me to come down and fill out an application in case any positions become available? Do you know of any _____(job title)_____ openings in the area?

> Or

> Would it be OK if I called back next week if you might have openings then?

Remember that communication is not just the words you use. Your Total Message Is:

- 7% Actual Words
- 38% Tone, Pitch
  - Volume, Rate
- 55% Body
  - Posture
  - Clothing
  - Facial Expressions
  - Gestures

You can find a more detailed guide to writing resumes and how to conduct yourself during an interview in the Resume Writing Secrets Guide. You can find a link to this guide at

http://www.felon-jobs.com/resources/

Bonding

There is a federal bonding program which will encourage employers to hire you. Ask your parole officer about this program. It allows companies to hire felons for jobs they might not normally be considered for due to litigation and insurance reasons. A school might never hire a felon normally but if the felony was not a violent crime and if the person can be bonded, the school may consider hiring him.

WOTC

Businesses often hire felons under the WOTC or Work Opportunity Tax Credit. Businesses receive tax credit when they hire felons under this program.

To see if the business qualifies, they need to complete IRS form 8850 before they make the job offer. They need to complete either a conditional certification form (ETA Form 9062) provided by the "new hired employee" or an individual Characteristics form (ETA Form 9061).

Then mail the forms to the Employment Security Department (WOTC Administrative Unit).

Suppose you want to work at one of three specific businesses. You know who the hiring managers are and their address but you are afraid they may not be interested. You can send them a letter that looks like a flyer on colored paper which says *TAX CREDITS FOR HIRING FELONS* which goes on to explain the benefits and the WOTC program. Then a few days later you can drop by with your resume. Now you have planted a seed in the mind of the employer that it is OK to consider hiring ex felons plus they may receive a tax credit if they do a good deed. Maybe they will look at your application more favorably.

Bureau of Prisons

The federal Bureau of Prisons bop.gov has information that can help you or your employer when it comes to hiring ex-cons.

http://www.bop.gov/inmate_programs/itb_employing_ex_offenders.jsp

On the above page you can find more information about the WOTC too.

You can find additional ex-offender employment resources here

http://www.bop.gov/inmate_programs/itb_references.jsp

Felony Letter Of Explanation

When asked if you have been convicted of a felony, you should never just answer YES and leave it at that. The interviewer's mind will assume the worst and that will be the end of your application process.

Have an explanation already printed and handy to hand the interviewer. There is something more official about seeing it in black and white even if the interviewer knows you printed it yourself. When you apply for a job, all the application says is "*have you been convicted of a felony*". It never asks what the felony was or what the circumstances were. If the FBI was looking for your brother and you panicked and lied about where he was and were then charged with lying to a federal agent, then that is not exactly a crime that will make people run from you in fear. A simple explanation can help if your crime is not a violent crime.

Your letter should honestly state your record(time served may be optional but if it was only probation that is good so list it). You need to take responsibility for your actions and acknowledge the effect it had on others. Talk about the way things have changed as well as what you have done since the crime not only for yourself but for your family. End by mentioning incentive programs available to the employer if he or she chooses to hire you and especially end with a positive sentence or two. Keep the overall letter short, never over 1 page, and preferably one half page at the most.

Here is a sample letter:

> In Jan 2000 I was convicted of _____
> _____. I served 18 months at _____ as a
> result. I have had a lot of time to consider my actions and
> I know that what I did was wrong. It was a result of poor
> decision making on my part and it hurt a lot of people.
> I've learned a great lesson and will never repeat those
> past mistakes.
>
> While incarcerated I worked as a _____ and I

achieved certifications in _____. Since my release I have worked part time as _____ and volunteered my time at _____. I am looking forward to returning to a fulltime position so I can further demonstrate the changes in my life and be a responsible member of society.

I can understand why you may be hesitant to hire someone with my background. However, I am eligible for The Federal Bonding Program which can insure you against any act of dishonesty on my part. Additionally, if you hire me, you will be eligible for Work Opportunity Tax Credits to save you some money this year. I will be happy to provide you more information about those programs when we meet. My experience in the field of _____ makes me an excellent choice for this position and my skills in _____ can benefit your company.

If your criminal record is several years old, with no recent convictions, and you have worked since your release, replace the paragraph about time served with one about what has happened since you were released. This should highlight your newly established work history. Also, remove mention of the Tax Credits from the last paragraph as this only applies for felons within a year of release.

Do not send this letter with every resume submission. This letter should only be provided in person at an interview and only when the issue of your conviction comes up.

> *NOTE: Do not put your conviction on your Resume. If you are applying at a company you expect to conduct background checks, then mention it in your cover letter. They will find out eventually so you might as well be upfront about it and bring it up when you are in control. If it pops up later, it will look like you were trying to hide something.*

If you apply for a job online, there is usually an option to include any additional comments or attach a cover letter. You can try applying without the explanation. If you do not hear back from the company in a reasonable time, then re-apply online but this time copy and paste your letter of explanation.

This letter can easily change what would otherwise sound horrible into a controllable business discussion. You are no longer left to the interviewer's imagination if he only had a one line summary to rely on. A summary from a background check may say"Falsifying Documents" and their imagination would run away with the worst possible scenario of you at the head of a massive driver's license counterfeiting ring. Your explanation about signing a form telling a federal agent that your brother left the country when he did not because you were afraid he would go to jail can help them understand what really happened which is not something included in a criminal history report.

In your letter you should never claim to be wrongly convicted. No one is going to believe you. Accept it and move on. Saying you were wrongfully convicted or that the police were out to get you or that you are still fighting the conviction will not help your chance at obtaining a job even if it is true and even if you have a video tape proving it. Just say what happened, you were convicted, and now you are putting your life back together and again, give concrete examples of what else you have done to achieve this goal.

The only possible exception to this rule is if you are trying to find employment with a group that would be sympathetic toward your situation. If you threw red paint on a woman with a fur coat and were convicted of felonious assault, then you might be able to use this to your advantage when applying at an animal rescue facility. They may not approve, but they would understand.

Be careful what words you use in your cover letter and during the interview. Never say "I am a felon", instead say I was convicted when I was younger or "I had a conviction several years ago." which puts it in the past tense. Remember, most people have no idea how the justice system works. They do not know the difference between a felony and a misdemeanor
40

or a traffic ticket. So, don't give too much information either. The less they know about some areas the less they can hold against you. You want to give them enough information to hire you but you do not want to explain the criminal justice system either. If they assume that you served your time and you are a regular citizen again because they do not know that a felony stays with you, then let them think that.

Also keep in mind that every ex-con who comes through the door of the hiring manager says "It was all in the past" or "I am off drugs now" so don't bother with such trite statements by themselves. They just lump you in with the other people who were not hired. Come up with better statements and combine them with concrete examples of how you have changed.

You DO want to discuss your conviction. You never want to go through an interview without anyone asking and be hired only to have your boss discover six months later that you are a felon. Now he will feel like you deceived him and will want to fire you which might not have happened if you had been upfront and explained the situation during the interview.

Also remember that you may not get a job and it may have nothing to do with your conviction. The company may have another person with more experience applying or an old college chum of the interviewer may have applied and in the interviewer's mind, the job is already assigned. Even without a conviction, you will not receive every job you apply for. There could easily be 20 other people applying and if three of them are qualified plus you, that only gives you a 25% chance of being hired anyway.

If you submit your resume instead of asking for an application then you have control over the information the company has. They may not even ask you to fill out a regular application. Some companies only use applications for low level jobs where the person is applying for a manual labor position and does not have a resume. Using a resume gives you control. You may have to fill out an application later, but in small and medium sized businesses they may never look at it.

Common Scams That Target Felons

If you do an Internet search for "felon jobs" then you can find page after page of these scams. Companies setup websites which look like they are offering jobs but they actually are regular job sites where you have no hope of finding employment anyway.

Some offer work-at-home jobs but then want you to pay them for the equipment needed, or want to charge you a membership fee or consulting fee, or they want to sell you a website where you can resell their products or some similar scheme.

Here are some common scams:

- Survey scams – no one will pay you to take a survey.
- Work at home scams – The companies pushing worthless work at home jobs often re-edit their sales pitch to target specific groups like ex-felons looking for jobs. Any and all of these jobs which claim you will make a fortune assembling goods, reselling items from the company etc are FAKES and SCAMS:
  - assemble items at home for big money
  - process medical billing at home
  - re-ship packages from home
  - copy names from the phone book
  - home based telemarketing
  - 900 numbers
  - envelope stuffing
  - Mystery Shoppers Wanted

and many more are SCAMS!

How the survey scam works: You spend all day filling out forms to make $10 then your emailbox is flooded with spam and they start calling you on the phone wanting to sell you worthless merchandise and other get-rich quick schemes. Many of the surveys are fake, they are nothing more than sales letters and the survey is a way to trick you into reading it thinking you might get paid or might win something. No one wins, it is a scam. In the end, you spend a lot of time filling our surveys and get less than minimum wage plus most of the companies will only give you a coupon which means you have to buy something at an inflated price to get your money. It is true that some companies pay for surveys, however they do not pay just anyone. They only pay certain people, such as IT managers at big companies, to fill out highly detailed surveys. Average people, those without high level experience in a field who are not well known for that experience, will never be paid for a survey like this.

Posting your resume to any of the resume sites is an invitation to scammers. The instant your resume is posted you will receive a number of job offers. These are scams. They are either trying to trick you into revealing your personal information or they want to trick you into doing something illegal. These professional scammers put up nice looking websites, they may even have phone numbers that look like they are in the US but they are not in the US. The entire thing is a scam to trick you into giving them your social security number so they can steal your identity. The other scam is when they want to hire you to do something like re-ship packages(which are filled with fraudulently obtained merchandise) or they want you to act as their US contact office and ask you to setup a bank account for the company etc. This is another scam which can land you in jail. No one in another country will hire you like this. There are legitimate job opportunities with foreign employers such as in freelance work through the Hire-Me Network, but you never have to reveal your personal information to them and foreign companies have no need for your social security number. Anyone who contacts you and claims they are in a foreign country and wants to hire you directly through an email is trying to scam you. Some of them are very polished and they say they have to do a background check or they must get approval but it is nothing but a trick because everyone gets the 'job'. Of course, there is no real job, it is just a lie to make you reveal your personal information so they can steal your identity.

Here is an example of one of the scam emails:

Dear Sir/Madam,

Our company is looking for permanent representatives within the territory of the Canada/United States of America and Europe. We need people at the age of 21 to 55 for rather easy work on processing of the incoming mail and parcels.

Candidate Requirements And Benefits:

- Have permanent Internet access
- An ability to pick up 5-30lbs parcels
- An ability to stay at home 3-5 hours a day
- Purposeful, responsible and vigorous person

The compensation is about $800 - $2000 per month.

Send your resume to our e-mail: xxxxxxxxxxxx@gmail.com

Thanks in advance as I look forward to hear from you for further information.

Best Regards
Steven Kaminsky
HR Manager

Anyone who accepted this job eventually found the police knocking on their door because this is part of an elaborate scam. The position described always involves basic skills, the chance to work at home, and little else. If you ever receive an email like this, it is a scam. No one is going to immediately offer you a job like this and no one needs 'general workers' with only general skills. Any company that contacts you and then provides a free email service like gmail.com, yahoo, hotmail, or any other free service as a reply address is a scam. Legitimate companies, even small companies, do not use free email services as their email address, they use their actual domain and their domain name should show that it has been registered at least 2 years at whois.net

Here is another with the subject *Mystery Shopper*. It is rather long so I cut out parts of it:

Thank you for your interested in the Mystery Shopper position.
Our company conducts surveys and evaluate other companies in order to help them achieve their performance goals.

....

Once we have a contract to do so, you would be directed to the company or outlet, and you would be given the funds you need to do the job(either purchase merchandise or require services), after which you would
write a rdetailed report of your experience.
Examples of details you would forward to us are:
1) How long does it take to get served.
2) Politeness of the attendant.
3) Customer service professionalism.
4) Sometimes you might be required to upset the attendant, to see how they deal with difficult clients.

.....

Requirements:
 * Must be 21 years of age or older.
 * Must have good written communication skills.
 * Must be able to focus on details.
 * Must have full internet access (at home or at work).
Mystery Shopping is fun and exciting but also must be approached very seriously and is definitely not for everyone.
If you are interested in applying for consideration as a Mystery Shopper do send in your information: michaelneilsen535@gmail.com

Full Name:
Address: City: State: Zip Code:
Phone Number: Age:
Occupation:

As soon as we receive your information we will add you to our database and we will look for locations in your area that needs to be evaluated.

Thank you,
Michael Neilsen

Once they have your information they will call and pretend to be a legitimate company by asking you regular interview questions, then say you are hired and ask for your social security number or ask you to fill out a form online that asks for your number. Any email that requests your name/address like shown above is a scam. Again, notice they used a free email address service here.

There are many scams targeting ex felons which offer work-at home opportunities that are fake, promise to remove criminal records and more. There is no resource that deals specifically with these ex-con scams but general resources explain how these scams work. They are the same scams all over the internet, they are just tailored to ex-cons.

You should sign-up for the free safety course at

<u>Auction-Safety.Org</u>

which will help you avoid not only eBay scams but many Internet scams.

Online Freelance work, like I already mentioned through Hire-Me sites, is by far the best option if you have any computer skills. It is a legitimate way to work for remote companies where you do not have to reveal your personal information to strangers. If you do decide to work for a fulltime company in the future, you can now honestly tell them that you have been doing freelance work for xx years and served xx clients who rated you 9.9 out of 10 and you can even show the potential employer your rating and history online. Now that is a powerful endorsement.

Criminal History Removal Scam

Beware of websites that claim they can have your conviction erased. Most of these websites only want to charge you an inflated fee. Then they will tell you they are working on it and to be patient until you stop calling. Some may tell you your conviction was removed when it was not. If you have a violent crime conviction or multiple convictions, your record will never be removed because no judge will approve of it.

A judge might approve if you have one relatively minor conviction and no other convictions. These companies charge you a filing fee and a processing fee(usually lumped in one big fee). Then they file paperwork for your record removal. That is all they do. Now whether or not a judge approves is another story. Some crimes may require the governor or the President to sign off on your paperwork and that will not happen unless you know the right people. These companies will not usually explain any of this to you, they only want you to pay for their service. They then have one of their workers fill out a form and mail it to the court with a processing fee charged by the court(which is much less than the fee they charge). You are better off having a free consultation with a local lawyer who can explain how it really works.

Other Options

Move

If you have a local or state conviction, you can move to a new state. Your records will remain in the old state. If you are subjected to a background check, it is unlikely your records will be found. Some services do check all states, but many basic background checks will only check your current state. Your application and approval for the background check form may ask where you have lived for the last 7 years so you may face the possibility of lying on it if your conviction was less than 7 years ago and you lived in the state where your record is located and you do not list that state.

Self Improvement

Life is a journey and everyone should work on improving themselves every day. Look into self-improvement courses of any kind, books, audio, video, any topic, anything and use them.

Do you constantly find yourself in conflict with management or other co workers at every job you take? If you are moving from job to job or find you are fired every 2 to 6 months, you may tell your friends that your boss was a ****** out to get you or your co-workers never liked you but you know that if trouble follows you everywhere you go, then you are carrying that trouble with you. If you constantly have conflicts then you must analyze what is happening, what you are doing that sparks the situation, and you may even ask your boss what you can do to fix it. He may not be the socially aware person who has the answer but if he can, he will help. If he can't help, then look elsewhere. An outside view is often helpful. You should look at private counseling. Your boss may even pay for it! There are many private counseling centers which will help you get along with others, reduce anger, and improve your performance at work. If you have such a problem, going to a new job will never solve it. You must identify the problem and find someone who can help you solve it. If you do not take steps to solve the problem then you will carry it with you to every job you take.

Drugs

I am sure you have heard this before, but there is no such thing as recreational drug use. If you use drugs then it will impair your performance at work and when your boss finds an excuse to get rid of you, he will take it. Your ability is impaired and your behavior changes even if you do not notice. Others will notice. Even if you only use drugs on the weekend or in the evening, even if that drug is alcohol, it will affect your work performance in ways you do not realize throughout the week. It affects your behavior, attitude, and actions even when it is not in your system because you are thinking about, talking about it, planning the next time. Any drug use, including alcohol, will make your life and your job more difficult.

> I had a friend once who only used drugs recreationally, marijuana was his choice. He could not hold a job and ended up at 43 years old as a pizza delivery boy. He would take a job and try hard but somehow he never

had time to actually do the job he was hired to do. It was always "I'm going to get right on that" and by the end of the day it was not done. Eventually he was fired until he took a job of delivering pizzas which meant someone handed him a pizza and told him to deliver it. That was the only way he could work, when someone stood over him and told him exactly what to do and he had to do it right then. He could never work on his own and get anything done. He could not pay his mortgage and never had any money to buy the things he wanted because he spent what he made on marijuana. He tried to go to school and took a student loan but he could not pay it back and defaulted. He was upset that the loan company had the nerve to call him wanting their money back so he decided because they were unfairly asking for their money back he would never pay it. It was always someone else's fault that he was in his situation. He lived in a run down house with rats and bugs because he spent his time smoking marijuana, hanging out with his friends, and playing computer games and not doing the normal things people do like picking up around the house, washing the dishes, mowing the lawn, going to work. Conditions became worse and worse but he continued along the same path and blamed everyone else for his problems.

At age 41 he died of a heart attack brought on from his use of marijuana and smoking cigarettes while neglecting his health by spending all of his time and money focusing on drugs. Don't be like my friend. Work on improving your life every day.

What Next?

Where are you now?

If you are still under a supervised release program, then following the direction and assistance given by a parole officer is most prudent. Follow it to the letter. Do not assume that something will be OK just this once. Either do not do it or ask first. Any rules you are given are absolute, there is no leeway, no fuzzy area, no maybe, no exceptions. At this stage, your primary goal is to complete your probation or parole, after which you may begin your new life. If you absolutely need cash, and cannot market your previous skills, then strongly consider a temp agency that will hire you out, and pay you, on a daily basis as a manual laborer or if you have basic computer skills look at freelance work through a <u>Hire-Me Network</u> site(but take the video course first so you know how it works, these websites are free to signup at but I recommend paying for the video trainer before trying to use them).

If you are already past the supervised release stage, then it's time to rebuild.

Where you are not now!

Although it's disheartening, there are jobs you can't have and there are almost no exceptions. These include anything and everything that involves firearms, and explosives. Bonded positions, highly regulated and licensed positions, and most government jobs are off the prospective list as well. Most positions that involve working around minors are out too.

You will most likely find your new career in a small to very small company, where you will work closely with the owner, in your own business, or working freelance. Most small companies struggle to survive, and rely heavily on each employee they have. You will probably be working with or near the owner, because they are working in the trenches to keep their company afloat on a daily basis.

Most medium to large companies don't want to be involved with any real or perceived liability in hiring you. If this is the route you really want to pursue, then work toward adding a lot of positive lines to your resume between the time of your conviction and the time you apply. Do not lie on the application since you will be fired if they discover the lie but work hard and set goals you can achieve.

Unskilled and semi-skilled labor positions are high on a convicts new job list, as most employers need to keep these revolving door type jobs filled. Residential construction labor is a good starter job. You can build your skill level, increase your wages, and maybe find a long-term job with a contractor. At least it will pay the bills while you complete a home-study or community college course.

Assume you will have to discuss your conviction, and that a background investigation will be done.

Employers want to know that you have moved-on from your experience. A simple statement is all that's needed. "I was convicted of _____ , and have fulfilled my obligations to the Court and society. I know that crime is wrong, and I also know that I have to try harder, and be better than the average person. I am ready to do this." (Don't go into a tirade about how life has done you wrong, or that you're a victim etc. The above statement is clear, concise, and should be accurate.)

You will now need to prove that you are in fact trying harder. This is not accomplished by words but shown by actions.

Education is a must. If you need a GED, get one. Enroll in Community College classes and/or vocational courses, private courses, go to seminars, home-study, audio/video classes, everything. If you have a skill or specific kind of education, consider teaching Adult Education classes. You may even be able to rent a night classroom at your community college and teach a paid one night or week long class where you collect the money and rent the room from the college for the night.

Use counselors to help develop a new career path. Don't be afraid to seek help from others. If one person is not helpful then try someone else. Not every counselor is good and not every counselor is bad. You may need to try a few before you find one that can help you.

Use peer support to explore new career options. If your old friends are always into trouble, make new friends and stop contacting your old ones. If your family is always in legal trouble then you should separate yourself from those problem people.

Try to expunge your conviction. If your conviction is not federal or major then it only requires a lawyer filing some forms with the court so it is worth trying. The worst they can say is no.

Prevent future convictions. This is a no-brainer, but somehow it still needs to be said.

You have been given second chance with a permanent legal handicap. Try to earn what you need to live comfortably, then seek success in more than just monetary achievement. You may find monetary success follows.

Many communities have people who work as an Employment Specialist who have connections to employers and job positions that provide information on felony/work release jobs. A good place to register and check in with is your local Job Service or Employment Office, or a city office that helps with employment. When you call, ask specifically about anyone who works directly with felons, people with criminal backgrounds, or any other barrier you might face (language, drug problem, mental disability, physical disability, Veteran status, etc.).

In some areas parole officers are told not to provide assistance in finding jobs. There are many reasons for this. One is to prevent any kind of personal involvement with the parolee. Another is for the benefit of the parolee because this motivates you to find your own solutions which will hopefully be better than a canned solution given to every parolee. When you have a number of restrictions that prevent you from doing normal job hunting (such as home confinement, not able to drive, monitoring bracelet, etc) then things get complicated. Again, this is why I recommend freelance work through Hire-Me Network sites. This freelance work is the one job that you can do from home and does not require a car, only a computer and Internet access.

1. Do not apply with placement agencies. These people have no interest in you. You will not generate any money for them, only headaches, so they do not want to deal with you. Some even trade information between themselves and say "this is a bad person, don't use him". They are under no obligation to remove old data on you after a period of time. Save them for the far future after you get a few years of work under your belt. Never pay for job placement. It is the employer who pays companies to find you. Any company that wants you to pay them to find a job is trying to scam you.

2. Apply direct. You can use the online employment services but stick with the big ones that you know are legitimate. Even here job listings are not checked so you should still be wary of anything that sounds too good to be true. Avoid the temptation to email your resume to everyone too. Be careful, many of these so called employers are really placement firms posting fake job offerings to lure you into contacting them so they can sell you to the companies you might have found online anyway. They may try to get your information for other marketing schemes and start calling you with work-at-home job offers that are scams, get-out-of-debt offers, or criminal-record-removal offers none of which are related to their job posting. Always check the name of the company and throw that into a search engine to see if you can find their website. Also make sure their website has been registered at least 2 years, you can check at whois.net and again, beware of anyone using free email services to hide who they are.

3. Apply to state and federal agencies. They have to hire you if you qualify. Your conviction should not count against you unless hiring someone with a conviction would violate law, or prevent you from getting a security clearance.

4. Check the local news papers online. Check the local papers and click the classified sections. Most will allow to you get to them for free, or you can read the paper at the library.

5. Check for local job fairs.

6. Check your local Yellow Pages for the names and addresses of companies that you think would have jobs for you. Call them to find out who to send a resume to and if they have any jobs open, then send a resume and cover letter. You can also drop off your resume in person, in an envelope, at the front desk.
7. Network with other people. Talk to your pastor, friends, relatives, anyone that could put in a good word for you.
8. Apply smart. It is not about applying for as many jobs as you can until you get lucky and someone accidentally hires you. It is about targeting your time and effort to jobs you can reasonably get that are also jobs you want. When you are not working, then your job is to find a job and that is what you should be working on at least 5 to 6 hours a day.

Second ID

You will need a second picture ID besides your state issued driver's license or state ID card. If you attend college then you will have one from them. You can also apply at membership clubs like Sams Club or Costco. They will require ID but if you have an old business card with your name on it, that is usually good enough to get a membership card from one of these club stores. You can apply for a passport which will have your photo in it. Many shops that take passport photos also offer ID cards. These are not as good as an ID card from a known company or college but they can be better than nothing.

Sex Offenders

In general, if you were a convicted sex offender you should seek a job that minimizes your contact with the public. This is simply common sense. If there should be a problem, and when you deal with the public some problem always comes up, your record will work against you. By minimizing your contact with the general public and never meeting customers in private places, you minimize the chance of trouble. Again, this is another reason I recommend freelance jobs through Hire-Me Networks because you never have to deal with anyone face to face, so it is perfect for sex offenders who need income but have difficulty finding employment.

After You Have A Job

After you are hired you should keep your conviction to yourself. Do not talk about being in prison or the crime, the unfair justice system, the police, or anything related to it with your co-workers. It just sounds bad for one thing and it can make people, who would otherwise like you, distrust you. The human resources person may not have told any other employees so they would not have known and now will think differently of you. When other management people hear about your conviction they may feel the human resources person is falling down on the job and complain. Now he is in a bad situation and he will look for the first chance to fire you just to get rid of you. When they need to lay off employees, you will be at the top of his list because your discussion of your criminal history made him look bad and caused him to be embarrassed for hiring you.

If your Parole Officer needs to contact someone, he can often contact the human resources person so that even your supervisor may not need to know about your conviction.

Remember that this job is not the job you will have for the rest of your life. This is just a temporary job to generate money until your conviction can pass into the past a little farther. You do not want to move from one low paying job to another either. You should keep jobs for 2 years. No one will want to hire you if they think you will quit in 6 months and they will have to find a replacement.

Work on improving yourself. I mean more than just moving past drug or alcahol problems. I mean true self improvement in every area of your life. Read self-improvement books, listen to audio programs, whatever you can and try to make one improvement in your life and in who you are as a person every day.

When you are first out of prison, you will simply have to suck it up and accept that for a while you will be subject to unfair treatment. In time your record will fall deeper into the past as you establish community connections and business relationships again. If you are at a job you do not like, stay there until you can find a better one and you know for sure you can quit the first. Then be nice and professional when leaving. As you change jobs every year or two you can move up and up until you finally reach the level you want to be at.

There is much more that you need to know when you come out of prison, more than just finding a job. This information has been compiled in another eBook which is free and described below.

Subscribe to the Daily Tip Sheet and receive an additional FREE guide called the *Recently Released Prisoner Employment Handbook* which includes information on

What Should I Do to Prepare for Release?
What about Federal Programs to Help Ex-offenders?
What about State and Federal Jobs for Ex-offenders?
What about Loans and Grants?
One-Stop Employment and Training Services
Physical and Mental Disability Employment and Training Services
National Internet Resource Link
Adult Training Programs
Native American Employment and Training Program
Senior Workers Employment Program
Apprenticeship Programs
Employer Tax Credit Programs
Welfare-To-Work
Federal Bonding Program
Other Programs Not Directly Related To Employment
Credit Reporting
Food Stamp Program
Public Housing
State Government's Interactive Chart of Re-Entry Housing

Options
Homelessness Programs
Social Security Administration
Domestic Violence Issues
Medical Assistance
Children and Families of Adult Offenders
How Do I get my Driver's License?
Inmate Bank Accounts
Ex-offender Voting Rights By State
Expungement of Criminal Records

You can subscribe to the Daily Tip Sheet which will have more employment information to receive the Recently Released Prisoner Employment Handbook for free at
http://www.felon-jobs.org

I have put a lot of research into compiling this guide and I hope the information helps you or your loved one.

Michael Ford
President Elite Minds Inc.

Additional resources are updated regularly at our website, go there now:

http://www.felon-jobs.com/resources/

Final Thoughts

I have mentioned self improvement a number of times in this book. I cannot stress how important it is. Many people stop learning after high-school and this itself limits their ability. You do not necessarily need to go to college or to take expensive home study courses to improve your skills.

Grammar - Improve your grammar and it will help you for the rest of your life. Improving your grammar is critical because you have to deal with customers, coworkers, and interviewers. If your grammar is bad then they will dismiss you as dumb and you will never be taken seriously when speaking or writing. Signup for this free grammar course to improve your grammar.

Reading Skills - Many people assume that how they read is just how they read and nothing can improve that. This is simply false. There are methods to improve how you read. Unfortunately, many teachers in the past have been unaware of these methods or they taught different methods that did not works as well. If you are a poor reader, you can still improve your sreading skills.

Learn Anything - Keep learning. There are countless free resources and low cost resources on the Internet that you can use to improve your skills, knowledge, and life. Never pass up a chance to improve yourself.

For more information and free links on these visit

http://www.felon-jobs.com/resources/

CPSIA information can be obtained at www.ICGtesting.com
Printed in the USA
LVOW10s1448110913

352007LV00015B/682/P